Glass Bricks

AT BAY press

WINNIPEG

Glass Bricks

LOUELLA LESTER

Glass Bricks

Design by Matthew Stevens and M. C. Joudrey.
Layout by Matthew Stevens and M. C. Joudrey.

Published by At Bay Press April 2021.

Library and Archives Canada cataloguing in publication is available upon request.

ISBN 978-1-988168-42-5

Printed and bound in Canada.

This book is printed on acid free paper that is 100% recycled ancient forest friendly (100% post-consumer recycled).

First Edition

10 9 8 7 6 5 4 3 2 1

atbaypress.com

To Mom and Dad, who taught me to work hard.

CONTENTS

Part 1 – Learning Work Ethic

Part 2 – Take A Risk

Part 3 – More Work Ethic

Part 4 - Using Every Skill You've Ever Learned

Part 1

Learning Work Ethic

Suck It Up

10 years old

I drag brush from the edge of the lawn, through the woods, to the top of the sand cliff above the beach. Mosquitoes cling to my ankles and toes, their venom sometimes paralyzing my skin until it's too late for me to notice and slap them away.

Years later, I take an art-history course and the professor lectures about eighteenth-century British landscape artists and how their paintings popularized a tame, sanitized version of the wilderness. I think of my mother, expanding the lawn a foot each summer, breaking lawnmower blades on the rocks hidden in the tangled grass at the edge of the yard. She grew up on the Prairie, married into the Shield, then started her not-so-patient expansion into the bush along the shores of Lake Winnipeg. It was slowed by breastfeeding, diapers, runny noses, and heating bathwater on a wood stove. Slowed to what must have felt like the speed with which the lake tips south as the land rebounds when the weight of the melting glaciers lifts.

Mom makes up for lost time as we grow older and she is able to assign us jobs. A ten-year-old might be able to wield an axe, chop down saplings. She supervises and reigns in her workforce. She weeds out my middle sister who is better suited to indoor chores. Then she can send my oldest sister and me, who are more adept at yard work, outside on our own.

On my way back from dragging brush, I spy a gnarled spruce. The swollen sap pimples on its trunk mimic the bites dotting my legs. I don't stop, but take note of that tempting tree, planning to return with a sharp stick to poke, pop and set sap running, once duty is done.

Frozen Eyes

Back in 1932, one of my great uncles traps two wild mink along the shores of Lake Winnipeg and attempts to breed them before he realizes they're both male. He works that problem out and it's the start of mink ranching in Victoria Beach, the small village where I grow up. Soon my grandparents, aunts, uncles, and cousins are building sheds to house the animals — they become mink ranchers who supply fur for the fashion industry in Winnipeg and out east.

The mink are kept in wood and wire pens, lined up inside the long peaked-roof sheds, within the fence-enclosed ranches. Sometimes mink squeeze out between cage wires or nose open a cage door and make a run for the fence.

When I'm little, Grampa promises me a nickel for each escaped mink I'm able to catch. I hide in the tall grass along the inside of the ranch fence, waiting for a mink to try to sneak past. When one does, I grab it by the tail, run it to Grampa, holding it as far from my body as possible, to keep safe from its pee and sharp teeth. Young male mink are easiest, too heavy or lazy to reach up and nip my arm. Skinny old females are more tricky, beady eyes watching and waiting for the right moment.

I get a job at my aunt's ranch up the hill from our house. She often babysat me and my sisters at her home when we were small. She was always kind. Knowing we didn't have running water at home, she let us bathe in the big tub at her house. At eleven years old, I'm happy to work for her, but not always so happy to make mink feed.

We lug wooden crates of fish from the walk-in freezer that keeps the summer fish catch frozen and drop them beside my work station in the feed shed. The eyes of the fish, like the eyes in a da Vinci painting, follow my every move until I've fed them all, nose first, into the industrial grinder. I keep a watchful eye on my fingers as the metal auger catches, then splinters and crushes the fish. It doesn't smell too bad until the ground fish is thrown into a cooker to break it down — if it is eaten raw, it will make the mink sick. Sometimes I almost gag from the smell as I add dry cereal to the mix, then pull the handle to dump the feed into the carts which my aunt will later wrestle from shed to shed.

The squeal of cart wheels always sets the mink into a frenzy that whooshes through the aisle of each shed. Claws gripping wire, heads circling, the dizzy mink wait for the feed my aunt scoops out of the cart with an over-sized spoon, then plops onto the wire top of each cage.

The ranch smells of rotten leftover fish, mink piss and the shit piles that build up underneath the pens. In the spring, flies lay eggs that hatch into squirming white maggots. In whelping season, this stench is mixed with the scent of hay packed in the wood nesting boxes at the front of the cages. But during this, my favourite season, I hardly notice the smells as I'm busy peeking into the boxes to count the number of squirming baby mink.

During the late-fall pelting season (my least favourite season) the village of Victoria Beach stinks of dead and dying mink. The nervous animals release a musk that's not as strong as skunk, but still unpleasant and the pungent odour cloaks the village like guilt. Ranch workers wear tough leather gloves to transfer scrabbling mink from cages into connected wood boxes. Carbon monoxide is pumped in through a hose running from a vehicle into the boxes.

The dead mink are gutted and the pelts are pulled up over their heads and turned inside out like quickly doffed wool sweaters. They are stretched, still inside out, onto long boards that have been sanded smooth to protect the fur. They are left outside for a while in cold weather or put in the walk-in freezers because it's easier to scrape fat from frozen pelts.

Once scraped, the pelts, still stretched over the boards, are hung to dry from hooks in sheds and basements. When my sisters and I visit my cousins we play in the basement near the pelts and at first I stay away from them. Gradually my nose gets used to the smell and I join in the games, running between and under the pelts which swing as we run through and then settle back into place after we have passed. When everyone else rushes upstairs for snacks, I stop at the bottom of the stairs, turn back and look at them hanging there like still pendulums.

When the pelts are dry, they are removed from the boards, soft fur right side out, and boxed for shipping. The boxes of pelts are taken south to Winnipeg to be auctioned off to buyers from all over Canada and the world, who will fashion them into hats, coats and stoles that I will never wear, nor will I ever want to. The city people dressed in mink don't understand where that fur comes from.

Bosses Are Fallible

5 years old

Household chores are more complicated when you have to pry chopped wood from the pile outside, haul it through the kitchen, pull open a door cut in the floor, and carry it down the rickety steps into the cellar. When you have to run up and down all day to refill the welded-barrel stove that heats the house. When the water pipe from the well across the yard freezes in winter months. When you have to fill your water pails outside and heat them for bathing, cooking food, or brewing tea. The kitchen refrigerator is no taller than my five-year-old self. The chest freezer, filled with frozen garden vegetables, is too big for the kitchen so it sits filling one end of the bedroom you share with two sisters.

Mom makes most food from scratch, boiling hand-pinched perogies, frying kibbi patties, and baking bread in the temperamental wood stove. Sometimes her voice is soft like the damp pie dough scraps she hands me to pat into a kid-sized tin plate and sprinkle with sugar and cinnamon. Other times her voice is dry and hard like the stale bread crusts she leaves on the counter for me to crush into stuffing crumbs with the heavy wooden rolling pin.

Screen Door

The wood outlining and bisecting the screen door is painted green to match the trim, accenting the building that's designed to look more like a cottage than a restaurant. The backdoor's coiled wire spring is curled too tight and it cracks closed behind me, nipping the back of my heel, clipping my elbow and knocking a few fish fly skeletons to the step below.

The boss pokes his head in. "What's that?" He doesn't trust a thirteen-year-old.

"Oh nothing, I just opened the door to let out a wasp."

"Make sure the door's hooked, eh?"

When I sneak back in after my clandestine cigarette I shut the door and squeeze the hook into the eye without making a sound. The boss won't let me forget that his wife once left the door unhooked and some punk sneaked in and stole a bag of mozzarella, most of it found later strewn along the path to the beach, crows fighting for the spoils. He often tells such stories, while his wife rolls her eyes behind her glasses, behind his back.

Lately when he talks I don't listen too much beyond his work instructions: his voice is just sound drifting through water. It's been this way ever since the night I came in with friends and ordered a grilled cheese sandwich. While we waited, I glanced over and saw the sandwich fall to the floor when he removed it from the grill. He didn't see me watching as he picked it up and plated it. I couldn't bring myself to say anything, but I only pretended to eat it, hiding it under a paper napkin on my plate.

This summer-only restaurant is quiet on weekday afternoons. The women cottagers are either sunbathing in cottage yards or lounging on screened-in porches while mother's helpers, like my middle sister, tend to their children on the beach. Their husbands, who migrate to the cottages on weekends only, are still in city offices where I imagine them chasing secretaries around desks, pinching bottoms, and whispering flattery. My oldest sister, walking through the brush along the sandy cliff road, once saw one of our uncles in the back of his car with one of those ladies, the one who always stuck up her nose when I served ice cream to her children. These husbands are surely unaware that their wives are sometimes enjoying what local people call "a little bit of rough," meaning local guys, the guys whose muscles bulge under their sweat-stained T-shirts while they clear brush from yards, patch cottage roofs, and wait for invitations.

There's no air conditioning in the restaurant. Sweat collects on my forehead as I weigh toppings and warm up the pizza oven, prepping for the supper rush. I shuffle to the screened window, hoping to catch a bit of a breeze. Dust clings to the fryer grease dulling the corners of each tiny mesh square, tempting the flies to buzz about searching for a way in. Teens, returning from the beach smelling of coconut oil and bug spray, flash by in the fluorescent oranges and lime greens of their bikinis and towels. I spot them between the saplings lining the shortcut path to the restaurant. Those teens were still asleep this morning as I pedalled to work on my too-small banana-seat bicycle from my home on the other side where more locals live.

The boss calls the first order. I pull a dough shell from the freezer, paint it with tomato sauce. Sweat threatens to drip from my chin and salt the pizza. I raise my arm, hesitate for one second, then safely wipe it away.

Stay Awake

9 years old

Dad sits for hours in the bulldog Mack truck cab bumping along highways across Canada and up north in Manitoba, pulling trailers full of farm equipment — balers, combines — and building materials — steel and lumber. His ears buzz from the strain of listening to hockey games on a radio that has trouble competing with the engine's roar. His hands tingle from the steering wheel vibrations.

When he's home, I stand for hours beside him as he fixes the truck. I hand him wrenches, hold the treble light, and run errands. In the winter cold, I stamp my feet, awaiting approval, like a horse waiting for oats. No matter the number of jokes traded or the thickness of my mitts or the fleece in my boots, my fingers and toes get cold. Don't complain. Colder. Show grit. A burning sensation. Be tough. Then numbness: you're no longer aware of your fingers and toes. But that's when it can be most dangerous.

I Will Not Give Him a Name

In 1975, I'm in Grade 12, renting a room in a house in Selkirk. I attend school in the morning, then drive into Winnipeg to work afternoons at my dad's rented trucking and repair shop. I take phone calls, do paperwork, put tires on rims and help with other truck repairs. I try to be aware of the danger around me: overfilled tires can pop off rims and fly; wrenches can slip; hot engines can burn fingers.

1979 — *She is fifteen when he picks her up with her friend in Winnipeg. He has a gun. He drives them outside the city. He rapes and beats them. He trusses them with wire and leaves them for dead. But they do not die, not like the girl that he did the same thing to a few weeks earlier. I read the news stories, but do not realize who he is until my dad calls and asks if I remember him.*

1995 — *After fifteen years of fitness hearings, trials and appeals he is convicted. Kidnapping. Rape. Attempted Murder. First-Degree Murder. Sentenced to Life.*

2006 — *There are publication bans on the names of victims of sexual assault, but she asks the court to remove the one on her name. Tracey Walsh wants to tell her story so that he never gets out. She says she will be at every parole hearing. "I'm not his first, but I am his last, and I have to keep it that way. I have to." His application for parole is denied.*

2008 — *Tracey travels to be at the hearing, but he withdraws his request for parole. She is walking down the hall in the psychiatric facility where the hearing was supposed to be held and she sees him. He too is walking down the hall, with no escort other than another inmate.*

2010-2020 — *Parole hearings are repeatedly cancelled, or else requests for parole are withdrawn. He dies in jail.*

In 1975, the truckers are surprised to see me — a girl — working at the repair shop. They yap, makes jokes, hang about. I'm friendly to them all, nothing more. None of them interest me — too old or too redneck or not my type. I get used to them and they get used to me. I'm never alone with him, or any of the other guys for that matter. He doesn't stand out from the group one way or another.

Getting Away With It

4 years old

Mom sends my older sisters and me up to the sand hill when the blueberries ripen. Each of us carries a different container, sizes in accordance with our ages. Toddlers start with a small empty Cheese Whiz jar, grow up to a pre-school pint sealer, then a grade-school quart sealer and eventually to a pre-teen pail.

I hate picking berries, so the summer I'm four I come up with a plan. By stripping the plants of leaves along with the berries I am able to quickly fill the jar, leaving time for me to dally about and daydream before I take it to Mom. She frowns at the jar, half-filled with leaves and stems, thinking I'm not yet ready for the pint.

Wobbling

Dad, who would rather deal with the repercussions than ask for permission, buys a small restaurant-grocery store without telling Mom. It's not far from our home on the shores of Lake Winnipeg. Once the dust settles, they end up working there from dawn 'til dusk seven days a week. Eventually Dad builds on rooms and they live there, their squabbling echoing from back to front and front to back.

I'm just finishing up high school, not living at home, but I work there on weekends and in the summer after graduation. I take orders, serve food, and collect money at the till. Cottager parents ask their children what they want on their hotdogs. Customers line up behind them, patience as thin as potato chips, while Mom cooks and mutters at the lack of wisdom in allowing toddlers to select their own food.

Locals and cottagers alike love the place. Road and hydro crews stop in for the generous early bird breakfasts. We serve real french fries chopped thick from potatoes peeled in the back. Stews with quality beef and vegetables. Fresh homemade apple and blueberry pie.

Cottagers walk the aisles asking for things like kiwi fruit. Mom explains those types of foods don't sell well out here. They buy milk and other perishables, but complain about the prices, comparing them to the prices of groceries purchased at big city stores supplied with low priced truckloads. On rainy days the place fills up with beach refugees fleeing gloomy cottages. Children whining for toys, women craving books, men planning cottage improvement projects.

One day I fill three aluminum cups with ice cream, milk and chocolate sauce, hook them to the milkshake machine, then turn to another task. I hear a metal shriek and a liquid gurgle, look back to see them fall, one to the front and one to either side. *Shit!* Shit!

Mom is outside cleaning the window, yelling through the glass for me to stop swearing.

To hell with this, I think. I hitch a ride to Winnipeg with the mail truck down washboard roads, the slow moving driver's voice wobbling along with each bump.

Take Pride In Your Work

3 years old

"Stay back, be careful." Outside the edges of this photo wood chips fly. Dad waves his hand towards me, the one that's not holding the axe. He turns and finishes the chopping. I wait, ready, wearing my overalls. Then he says, "Now, you take this and put it on the woodpile." He hands me a piece, one quarter of a short round. Ready for the photo, I hold it high on my shoulder, my smile pulling a chuckle out between my teeth.

Part 2

Take a Risk

Is It Real?

We each drop a second hit after we start coming down from the first, then decide to go to the airport because someone said runway lights are really wild when you're stoned. I'm at the wheel, even though it's not my car, because I'm the only one who hasn't been drinking. I'm driving slow because it feels like we're weaving between lanes. I see a flashing red light coming up behind me and I panic, thinking the cops are going to pull me over for driving like a snake. I ask the others if it's real and they say it's really a cop. I pull over, but the police car speeds past us. (*Deep Breath*)

At the airport we stand in a row along a window staring out at the purplish runway lights until a security guy waves us along. Then we line up in the cafeteria and I see the lady at the cash register has a string of spittle running from her mouth all the way down to the till. When she moves to take money it quivers. I'm sure I'm hallucinating as I wait for it to break. I hear guffaws behind me and turn to see my friend holding one hand over his mouth. He nods his head, up and down. Fuck, what's the chance of that happening when you're on acid? We break down, laughing too hard to explain it to the others, and when we're finally able to, they don't believe us.

Darkness is about to pull away from the horizon when I get home. Home is a one-bedroom basement apartment I share with my oldest sister. She attends university while I work and try to decide what I really want to do now that I've graduated high school. We don't have much furniture. A card table and two chairs are cornered in the kitchen.

Another card table, holding textbooks and an always-full ashtray, serves as my sister's desk. It squats there in the bedroom, swaybacked, beside her foam pad bed. The only things in the living room are wooden soft drink boxes and a bean bag chair that does double duty as my bed. I lie there, still stoned and unable to sleep, anticipating the alarm clock. Then I give up and go to the kitchen to make breakfast.

When I try to eat my toast, it tastes like the cover of one of my sister's textbooks. I lie down again, head and shoulders resting on the beanbag chair, and run my tongue over the indentations in my back teeth. It feels like a mop swabbing a potholed highway. I place my hand flat on my chest, after I figure out which side actually holds my heart. It seems like it's beating way too fast. (*Deep Breath*)

The alarm clock goes off. I work at a joint gas station and car wash. I know I'm too stoned to handle the gas station attendant's duties, like charging credit cards or dealing with possible gas tank overflows.

The car wash attendant's duties, on the other hand, involve pushing the correct wash button, then hand-cleaning the license plates and door handles with a brush. The only thing that can go wrong is a mix-up when selecting one of three buttons: regular wash, spray wax or hot wax. Either way the car gets washed.

I'm always the first employee to arrive at work, even now when I'm still stoned, so I get first dibs on the jobs. This morning, I tell the boss I'd like to run the car wash. He seems a bit surprised by my choice, but says okay. (*Deep Breath*)

The First

The news in the 1970s: The CN Tower in Toronto is completed. Nadia Comaneci gets a perfect score on the uneven bars at the Montreal Olympics. Steve Jobs and Steve Wozniak form the Apple Computer Company. And I land on the front of both of Winnipeg's daily newspapers.

Male. Male. Male. Male. Male. Male. Male. Male. Male. Male. Male. Female. I wait along with hundreds of other trades students in this gym at Red River Community College. *Male. Male.*

On June 28, 1977, the *Winnipeg Free Press* headline quotes me saying, "I just like mechanics." I do like mechanics, but no more than anyone else and certainly not enough to warrant a headline. I cringe, realizing the headline could be read as a joke, and wish I'd spoken of mechanical pursuits. Running below that headline is a photo of me crouched beside an engine, wearing a short sleeve T-shirt under a denim overall, and the cutline says, "Louella Lester's graduation gift from her boyfriend was a new set of wrenches." Who's the hero?

A day later, the *Winnipeg Tribune* kicker, "First Woman" is followed by a headline with me saying, "Anything Possible." An unusual surge of confidence for me. But it's all girls in my family. Growing up no one told me I couldn't do something because it was just for boys. In that same article I'm quoted saying, "I couldn't really see myself sitting in an office." I have an aversion to offices because my mom, being a worrier, nagged me to take typing in high school so I'd have something to 'fall back' on. I refused, wondering what I might end up 'falling back' from. I didn't know I'd become a writer, spending hours two-finger typing at a desk.

Even before the man shouts, "Diesel Mechanics!" and we move forward, I notice a group of instructors staring right at me. *First. First. First. I'll be theirs. First. First. First.* When the instructor calls out my name — necks stretch, words become whispers and the crowd parts. *First. First. First.* Once we are clumped at the front, some classmates gawk while others attempt to play it cool. *First. First. First.* The boldest ask me questions like: "How come you're taking this course?" *First. First. First.*

The *Winnipeg Free Press* reporter lists my address in the article and calls me Miss Lester at a time when *Ms Magazine* already exists. In the article I say it wasn't a 'big women's lib thing' even though I do believe in equal rights and equal pay for women. I always helped my dad with yard work, building things and fixing trucks. I did quit wearing a bra back in junior high, not long after Mom bought me one, because it was so uncomfortable, and I ignored boys who made comments. But I'm young and don't want to be responsible for all women — fearing I'll let them down if I don't succeed.

The *Winnipeg Tribune* finishes with, "I sure wouldn't spend three or four years getting a degree." I later return to school to complete two degrees, then work for twenty-five years as a secondary school teacher.

Clap, clap, clap. At the graduation ceremony necks are stretching again as my fellow graduates' loved ones get a look at me. *Clap, clap, clap.* I choose to wear an overall, just a bit feminine, a sleeveless fitted white outfit with two red stripes running along the top above my bosom. *Clap, clap, clap, clap.*

At some point in 1977 a photographer takes a photo of me, along with a male student, rebuilding a transmission. It's the cover photo on the *Red River Community College - Diesel Mechanics-Transport* pamphlet for the next few years.

Mechanical Snippets (1977)

1

When I start working as an apprentice diesel mechanic at the age of nineteen, I'm the only woman in the shop. The wrench slips when I am loosening a cap screw one day and I jam my finger against the still-hot engine. "Fuck!" I say. The shop goes quiet for a moment, then the air relaxes and settles. Then I hear the disembodied voice of a quick-witted jokester from under a truck across the shop, "What a relief...she swears!"

2

We wear grey overalls or shop coats, which are sent for cleaning each week. Above the left pockets are tags with our names. I walk past another mechanic one morning and he says, "Nice name. What do you call the other one?" I follow his eyes to the name tag above my left breast. I'm not yet ready to take up these type of battles, so I smile and play dumb. There's something about him, a tendency to look for short-cuts — a laziness. I don't like him and usually manage to avoid him. Months later I notice he hasn't been around for days, but he often misses work so it's not unusual. I'm not unhappy when I hear he's been fired, though I do wonder if it might have happened sooner if I'd spoken up.

3

There's no women's washroom or change room in the shop, so someone attaches a hook to the wall in the secretary's washroom near the front offices. I hang my overalls on the hook at the end of the day and the secretaries clutch their skirts while giving the overalls a wide berth. I'm careful to rinse the sink clean after I scrub the grease from my hands.

4

The foreman hurries into the shop carrying a basket of fuel injectors. Following close behind him is another man, who I assume is the trucker attached to the parts. The foreman tells me he has a rush job. The injectors were fixed in Alberta, but something is still wrong and the driver has to be in Toronto tomorrow. He turns to the staring trucker, tells him I'll be looking after him, and takes off. "You're going to fix them?" asks the trucker.

"Yup."

"Ahh, do a good job, eh?"

"I always do."

He leaves for coffee and returns an hour and a half later. I show him the parts I replaced and explain what was wrong, saying he shouldn't have any problems now. He smiles and shakes my hand. "Well, when I go back through Calgary next week I'm going to stop at that shop and tell them a woman did a better job than they did."

5

All day we toil in shades of grey. Overalls. Concrete floors. Engines. Wrenches. Grease and oil. The only break in the visual monotony is the odd red truck cab or a peep of blue sky when the doors roll open to let a truck in or out. Every so often the foreman closes our whole shop early and we all file into the classroom to learn about engine changes, innovations and new techniques. It's nice a break from the usual. One day a woman, introduced as an interior designer, comes in to look around the shop. She soon disappears into the classroom that is to be renovated. A month later, when the decorators leave and the paint has dried, the walls are grey and the cupboards are a dark shade of grey but not as dark as the chairs in which we slump.

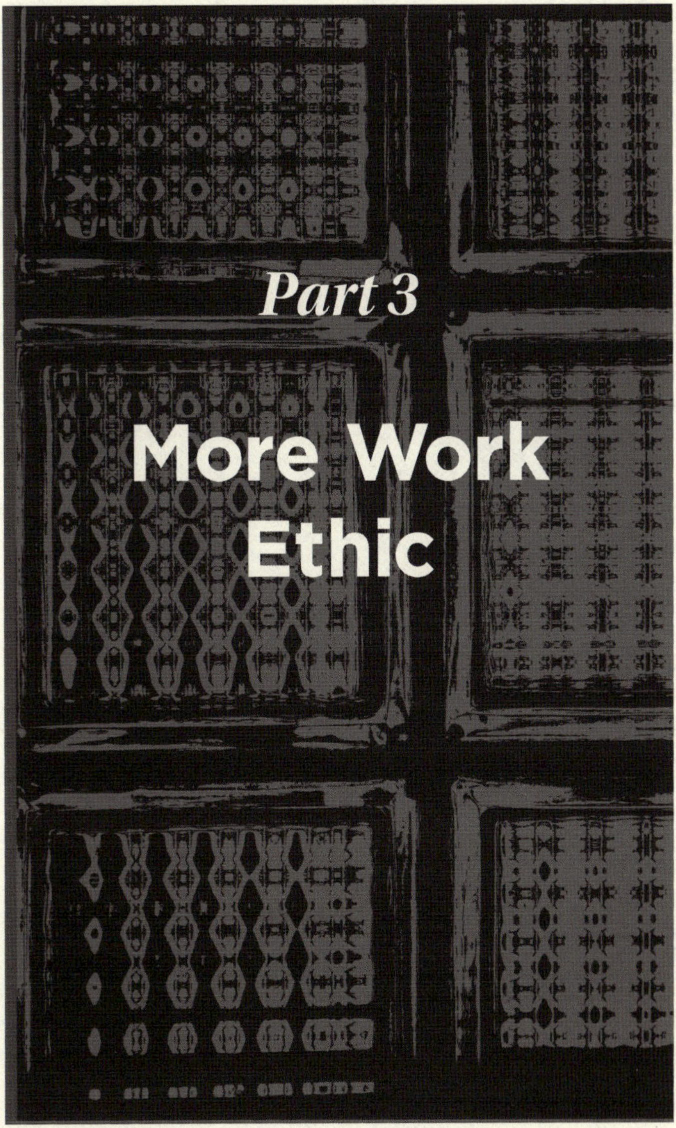

Part 3

More Work Ethic

Stick to Your Guns

4 years old

The .22 gun is as tall as me. It leans there in the shadows in the space between firewood cubbyhole and the wall, just inside the back door. It reminds me of a frozen deer leg, brown and wider on one end. Knowing it's empty doesn't make it less scary. I never watch when Dad uses it to shoot the ground squirrels that eat the young garden plants we depend on for food.

One day my sisters and I go to the dump with Dad and he brings the gun. I think he plans to use it to protect us if a hungry black bear comes around. I'm standing off to the side in the jack pine woods. My sisters are somewhere behind me. Something moves in the undergrowth — a prairie chicken strutting past a juniper bush. Crack! I jump and the startled prairie chicken tumbles to its side. I turn and Dad's still aiming the .22. I know it's for supper and, though it's the only option, even Mom can't make me eat that bird.

Solo Night Shift

On December 23, 1981, 16-year old waitress and high school student, Barbara Stoppel, was found strangled in the washroom of a Winnipeg donut shop where she had been working alone. She died a few days later. The wrong man was charged with the crime, but was exonerated after three different trials. Later, another suspect was found dead with a note declaring his innocence. The crime was never solved.

It's a busy Saturday evening at the 24-hour donut shop where I work on weekends while I'm in university. I mix icing for donuts. I dip and fix the dripping with a twirl of a fingertip, all the while keeping watch for customers. I smile while I read off the names of the donuts: chocolate, strawberry, vanilla iced, maple, crullers, jam busters.... Smile stuffing bags and boxes. Smile making change. Smile. I serve full cups and wipe empty counters in front of the crooked NO TIPPING sign. I stuff a jam-buster in my mouth. Slurp cold tea. Then run to the washroom between customers. Someone is always waiting when I return. I empty the dishwasher. Fill it, empty it. Fill. Empty. It continues like this until things slow down after 8pm.

When I'm alone in the donut shop, with damp coffee grounds and dried-out crumbs. I have time to catch my reflection in the window across from the front counter. Time to contemplate what might happen if I was to arrange for a friend to visit.

I'd set it up so he'd arrive right when I was about to open the till in order to follow the boss's instructions to count out the accumulated money but keep a small float before hiding the rest in the back & instead I'd hand all of the money to my friend & give him plenty of time to flee before I called 911 & when the cops showed up I'd muster a few well-timed tears while answering all of their questions & I'd describe the thief as looking different from my friend but not too different in case some unseen witness got a detailed description & the next day I'd wait to visit my friend's house until late afternoon in case the police were watching & we'd split the money & I'd spend some of my share on rent or a bus pass & maybe treat myself to a new pair of boots.

Business is slower than usual later on this Saturday night. A winter storm has called away all the tow truck drivers and most other customers. A lone cabbie enters. He's the one who used to ignore the NO TIPPING sign. Who once told me I didn't fit in at the donut shop. Who said I was destined for bigger and better things, right before he asked me out on a date. I said no. He has not spoken to me since. He still comes in on Saturdays. I serve his coffee: cream, two sugars. But now he places only the exact change on the counter beside his cup.

Sell Yourself

5 years old

After breakfast Mom calls my sisters and me to the garden. We pick lettuce, peas and beans while she digs baby potatoes, carrots and onions. We fill the red wagon and drag it to the well where we pull up pails of water to rinse the vegetables clean of earth and bugs. Then Mom organizes the wagon into green, yellow, orange and reddish-brown vegetable-filled quadrants until it looks like one of our grandmother's handmade patchwork quilts.

We leave the vegetables to dry in the sun while we pick the grime out from under our fingernails and change into clean clothes. Mom says she'll give us a dollar of the profits if we sell everything in the wagon to the cottagers who summer along the beach south of our house. We plan to sell everything for sure, and as we change, we discuss which penny candies we'll buy at David's store later in the day.

Before we leave Mom tells us what we should charge for the bunches of vegetables and gives my oldest sister a small bag with coins for making change. Then she tells us a story about our dad. When he was a young child his mother sent him to sell home-baked pies to cottagers. One woman cottager asked the price of the pies. "Twenty-five cents each," Dad said. The woman dipped her fingers into her change purse and handed him a quarter for one blueberry pie. "No," Dad said, "it's twenty-five cents." We've heard the story before but we still laugh. I'm pretty sure my oldest sister, who is good at math and is older than Dad was when that happened, won't make that kind of mistake.

While my middle sister and I follow, my oldest sister tugs the full wagon to the far end of the row of cottages. Then my sisters take turns knocking on doors. I'm shy and stay back behind the wagon, but I do enjoy shouting, "Fresh vegetables for sale! Lettuce. Peas. Beans. Carrots. Potatoes. Onions." The vegetables sell quickly and I change my shouts as we run out of certain vegetables. But when I have to shorten my shout to, "Fresh vegetables for sale. Onions," sales slow to a stop.

At the last couple of cottages people say they will buy carrots or potatoes if we have them, but not onions. Now my oldest sister stops smiling. She's walking fast and I'm having trouble keeping up. "If we don't sell everything Mom won't give us the dollar," she says, then stops in front of an A-frame cottage. She puts three onions in a crumbled paper bag and hands it to me. "Okay, you're going to go up to that cottage, but don't shout about vegetables, just shout that onions are for sale."

"Why do I have to go? I'll shout, but one of you guys should go."

"No, they'll buy from you because you're little. Don't you want us to sell everything so Mom'll give us a dollar? Go!"

I want that dollar. I want to buy candies. But my hands are shaking so hard I'm having trouble gripping the bag of onions. "Onions for sale."

"Louder. Go knock on the door," my middle sister says.

"Onions for sale!" my oldest sister shouts.

I tap at the screen door. A grey-haired lady leaning on a

cane peers down through the mesh. "Well, what have we here? Onions. Hmm. Onions. Let me get my purse. I don't really need onions, but you are such a cute little thing."

Get the Dirt Out From Under Your Nails

My roommate Wen lights up a hand-rolled cigarette, scratches his head, and tells me he's been hired by Martin — a graduating student who knows how to write up grant applications — who has created a project providing summer employment for four students.

The job involves writing up student travel information, mapping bicycle routes for student travellers, and negotiating student discounts at businesses throughout Manitoba. I'm intrigued by the idea of work that doesn't require physical labour, and the roommate connection gets me an interview.

I flick a nail file through the air as though it's a magic wand, rid myself of nervous tremors along with the dirt under my fingernails. My love of talk and laughter masks my lack of confidence. I get the job.

We work out of an office at the university. It's filled with filing cabinets, desks, and tables. Martin explains what he wants to accomplish, in general, what he wants us to do, then waves his hand toward the desks and tells us to get to it.

I work with Jen, a cycling enthusiast who makes self-deprecating jokes, and Dana, who has a heart of gold and a smile filled with perfect white teeth. At first, as we shuffle papers and share ideas, we balk at the latitude we've been given to think and create.

I take tentative steps towards a new confidence in my own capabilities.

Everyone Needs Company

11 years old

For years, Dad works as a long-distance trucker. Sleeping in cramped truck cabs, rather than expensive hotel beds, means he develops a habit of sleeping for only a few hours at a time. So when he's home, he's up before sunrise working on projects. Digging a drainage ditch. Fixing the truck. Building a new house, which takes a long time because he's only home weekends.

The puppy that came with visiting friends a couple of years ago is now a big black fur ball that lives outdoors. He stretches out on the cool gravel on hot summer days, in the hay-covered doghouse in the winter. He can sometimes be found in the summer cottage area humping purebred dogs while their horrified owners try to shoo him away. He buries bones in the bush, leaves them there until they're stinky-ripe, and then he brings them back to gnaw on the step. Not the type of dog who gets a bath, except in the lake. Not the type of dog who spends much time indoors especially after he got confused on his first Christmas and peed against the coffee table that stood next to the tree in the living room.

Outdoor dogs are excited to be indoors. Excited dogs jump on beds.

Pre-teens like to sleep in. Dad likes company.

Chewed Up and Spit Out

When I'm a kid I often chew paper, pretending it's fruity gum that has lost its flavour, until the day I'm caught. "Why are you chewing gum in class?" The teacher pretends he's asking a question. "You know the rules — stand up — spit it out and stick it on your nose!" But I can't because I've already swallowed it along with the explanation that won't stick either.

I know where paper comes from because I love to sit on the beach and watch tugboats pull log-filled booms across Lake Winnipeg. They bend and undulate in the air above the sun-heated water, the same way cars do over hot asphalt highways. Sometimes a single log escapes, rides the waves west, and lands on my shore ready to play at being a seahorse or a water dragon. But usually all the logs disappear into the Winnipeg River, head to the mill in Pine Falls where they'll be chewed, mixed with chemicals, and eventually spit out as paper.

In my early twenties I'm still having a hard time explaining my way out from under the weight of other people's suggestions. So, though I live in the city, I end up driving north to work weekdays with my dad at the pulp and paper mill.

Dad backs an empty tractor trailer up until it kisses the yawning loading dock. Inside the trailer, I grab the end of a thick metal band and snap it, sending a metal wave to the other end until it straightens itself. I do the same with the second one and together they mimic train track rails. I kick the wood wedges to the side and wait.

When I hear a distant hum I paste myself to the trailer wall, safe from the forklift that grasps a one-ton roll of paper in its jaw. Each roll, when standing end up, reaches at least to my chin. My arms cannot come near to encircling one. And my toes could never survive its crushing weight.

The forklift operator flips the roll on its side, sends it to the front of the trailer, then backs out and is gone. I rush to keep the roll from bouncing back, amazed that I can stop it so easily. I kick a wedge between its belly and the floor. We do this over and over until the trailer is full. I winch the metal bands tight across the rolls, like braces on a teenager's teeth, so the load, destined for a Winnipeg newspaper company, won't shift on the highway.

Dad moves the full trailer and hooks up to another empty one while the forklift idles and the forklift driver chews gum, or maybe it's tobacco. And I just wait.

Is The Cookie Worth It?

5 years old

I sit in my chair, feet dangling below crossed ankles, alone at the table. My left elbow is resting on the table's big scar — the scar Mom left there last winter when she missed while trying to chop up a frozen deer haunch with an axe.

I've eaten most of the stew — well, the gravy-potato-carrot part, and even the pea part. But just below my chin is the cold-fatty-gristly-stewing-beef part that I just can't yet bring myself to eat.

Mom's up on the hill picking the last batch of wild blueberries for this season. My sisters are doing dishes, as Mom told them to do before she left. I'm not helping because, even though I'm five now and old enough for chores, Mom has said I'm not allowed to leave the table until I finish my stew.

My sisters are laughing, making chewing sounds and saying how great the sugar cookies taste — a treat after they finished their stew. I'm trying, I really am, because I love sugar cookies and I know each one has a smiley-face made of crunchy almonds. I count the pieces of meat — one, two — all the way to five. I close my eyes, fumble to pick up the smallest piece, then pop it in my mouth. I swallow without chewing, swallow it quick, as though it's one of the big cod liver oil capsules Mom makes us take whenever she thinks we aren't eating right. I do this over and over until there's only one chunk left, but then I make a big mistake.

I open my eyes. And I see it, attached to the meat. A vein about the size of a small macaroni. I heave, almost throw up the other pieces, close my eyes, open them again and look at my sisters. They're busy, their backs turned. I pop the meat in my mouth and tuck it into my cheek. I heave as I stand up. "All done," I say before running to the bathroom.

In the bathroom I spit the ugly piece of meat into my hand, flip open the slop-pail toilet lid and throw it in there. I don't even close the lid when I leave, thinking the piece of meat will disappear into the watery waste. It's not until Mom comes back from the hill that I find out it didn't sink. I don't get the cookie.

Classical Conditioning

On his deathbed, Pavlov had a student sit beside him to record the circumstances of his dying. This required a lot of time and patience — similar to the time and patience needed for collecting dog saliva and recording the results while training dogs to anticipate food at the sound of a buzzer.

Before they invent direct-distance dialling, I work as a long-distance operator — watching a computer screen, wearing headphones, jumping to attention, and speaking at the sound.

Beep: *Operator may I help you?*

Beep: *Operator may I help you?*

I wait for payday, saliva building under my tongue.

You Can't Always Win

11 years old

The first thing I see when I open the fridge, is a plastic bag full of half-frozen pork chops. Mom works outside the home, so my sisters and I are expected to run things. Outside: mow grass, cut firewood, rake, weed the garden, pick vegetables and berries, and in the winter, shovel snow. Inside: dust, vacuum, sweep, mop, wash dishes, and cook meals. She has high expectations and very little tolerance for mistakes.

While I stand in the kitchen, my oldest sister comes home from high school and I show her the chops. "Do you think we should cook the pork chops for supper tonight?"

"Well, Mom left them out to thaw, so she must want us to cook them," she says.

"But they're only half-thawed. If she wanted them for supper tonight, she would've left them on the counter so they'd be totally thawed, wouldn't she? Maybe they're for tomorrow's supper."

We carry on discussing pork chops and no-win situations. Sure that we will make the wrong decision, we are only trying to gauge which mistake will get us into less trouble.

Effectively Directing Your Anger

Math class could never sustain my interest beyond the little shot of happiness I felt when, using only the teacher's example, I was able to figure out the solution to a problem.

* * *

When I am in my early twenties, I work at Canada Revenue Agency for one tax season. This is before it is called Canada Revenue Agency, and long before filing taxes online. We are grouped in stations, one worker at each of the four desks forming a square around a pole with an electrical outlet on either side. An electric stapler and an electric pencil sharpener are plugged into each outlet. There is space on the side of each desk for the bins which we pick up as needed from the next room. The bins are filled with completed tax returns still in their envelopes which have been slit open by a machine and packed according to type. Black-edged envelopes hold simple, straightforward returns and the grey ones hold more complcated, time-consuming returns.

* * *

I liked getting a final answer — a solution. But once I figured out a particular type of problem I quickly became bored. There was no little shot of happiness to be found in doing the same type of calculation over and over.

* * *

At first I enjoy the order and organization of this job. We open envelopes, sort the various T4 slips, forms, notes and schedules into a predetermined order. We are paid an hourly rate that increases based on the number of returns we complete. The bins of black-edged envelopes are popular because they can be organized more quickly. To promote fairness, the bosses enforce a rule that workers alternate between black-edged envelope bins and grey envelope bins. Some workers sneak in extra black-edged envelope bins to increase their return count, and their pay. The supervisors do not always catch these cheaters.

* * *

Then there are the disgruntled taxpayers. Their misplaced anger goes into their tax forms rather than through the proper channels. I never know what I will get when I open an envelope. Some taxpayers are creative. They slow us down — affecting our pay — by cello-taping or stapling excessively, paying their bills with envelopes filled with coins, attaching notes with various well-chosen expletives, and smearing food or nose pickings on the paperwork.

What You Don't Know Can't Hurt You

3 years old

After supper, Mom adds wood to the kitchen stove instead of letting the fire die down for the evening. She turns to my oldest sister. "Bring some extra wood from the pile inside the back door." Now I know it's bath night.

Mom sits the kettle on the stove, dips water from the big pail into it, then tops up the reservoir on the side of the kitchen stove. She makes her way down to shove more wood into the homemade steel-barrel stove in the basement. She pants back up the stairs carrying the square metal tub, which she slams onto the kitchen table with a grunt. Mom moves back and forth between the kitchen stove, water pail and tub. "Okay, you're first," she says. And she's looking at me.

I love bath time, especially because Mom always goes from youngest to oldest and at three years old I'm first. My feet are cold from the icy linoleum because the basement stove has not yet had time to reach its warmth up to thaw the kitchen floor. Mom picks me up and I dip my toes into the warm clear water, no suds yet. She lets me sink into the tub and once I'm sitting in it I just can't help myself — I need to pee. My sisters, whose baths will follow, won't know, so when Mom's back is turned I go ahead.

Fifteen years later, my sisters and I, now all university students, sit around a kitchen table in the old house we rent in Winnipeg. I confess to my oldest sister, who was always the last to bathe, and we all laugh. Then our middle sister says she did the same thing. My stomach hurts from too much laughter. I gasp, my hand holding my belly. But I see my oldest sister has stopped smiling. "Think of it this way," I say, "it could be the reason — you have such — smooth — blemish-free skin."

Quick Money

My good friend Wen sits alone, skinny and tipping back in his chair — only the back legs touch the ground. His eyes squint through the smoke dancing up from his hand-rolled cigarette and under his wire-framed glasses. He holds a beer bottle in his hand.

Steve smiles, rides the smoke across the room, introduces himself to Wen and asks for a drink and a cigarette. Wen understands those needs and has a soft heart, so he says yes and offers a corner of his table — the friendship later cemented out back over a shared joint.

Steve explains he's been squatting in a "vacant" apartment building downtown near the university, a building recently taken over by a bank. A man has been sent to clean out the building, to make it ready for sale to someone who might fix it up enough to attract student tenants. The man meets Steve, likes his smile, and is impressed by an unapologetic squatter who knows the importance of a handshake. He says he'll pay him under the table to do the job, but gives him a deadline one person alone can't meet.

Wen introduces my boyfriend and me to Steve at a party. Steve tells us he's on the run. He's worked his way east, from BC to Alberta to Saskatchewan to Manitoba, wanted by the law and others, he says, in a couple of those provinces. I don't ask why, because I think I know: drunk driving, drug sales, robbery, drunken assaults. He reminds me of what some of the guys I knew in my teens would be like if I was to run into them now. They are good guys when sober.

I'm attending university, and it's the between-student-bursary-and-income-tax-cheque-time — or maybe the between-income-tax-cheque-and-summer-job-time. Either way I'm broke. Steve asks if I want to help him meet the deadline. I say yes.

The next day, my knock wakes him, but a grin is crinkling the corner of his eyes when he opens the door. He's wrapped in an unzipped sleeping bag that also serves as a bed. He points for me to sit in one of the two kitchen chairs, facing each other in the living room, separated by a tinfoil ashtray with butts spilling onto the floor. Empty beer bottles crowd the kitchen counter and stovetop. He picks some off one of the elements to make room for a pot of water, before he goes into the other room to dress.

When he returns he offers me tea. He's wearing his usual faded t-shirt, jeans and jean jacket. He fills two cups with boiling water and dips the same teabag into each. He offers me a cigarette and lights it before he passes it over. I try to ignore the floaty things on the surface of the tea and the stains on the rim of the cup. I smoke the cigarette, raise the cup to my lips, pretend to drink. When Steve goes to the washroom I pour the tea down the drain without making a sound.

He gives me garbage bags, rubber gloves, liquid cleaner, rags, a broom, a mop and a pail. He tells me to do "just enough." We climb to the third floor and start on opposite ends.

The door of the first apartment won't close all the way: the upper hinges are bent and the screws are missing. Fist-sized holes are evenly spaced at the exact same height all the way down the hallway.

In the living room, the morning sun, blurred by the fingerprint smudges on the windowpanes, attempts to brighten the scratched oak sills and baseboards.

I don rubber gloves in the kitchen, pull soggy paper plates, plastic forks and a plastic bag half-filled with mouldy bread from the sink. I sluice the basin with the liquid cleaner and wipe out the worst of it before I plunk the pail in and fill it with hot water. I swipe at the stovetop, knocking what I think is black burnt rice to the floor, until I see a petrified mouse curled up under an element.

I open the fridge before I realize it's been left closed and unplugged for some time. A thick smell bursts out and I almost trip as I quickly back away. Nothing in the fridge is recognizable except the pizza box. A green-black sludge has dripped down to settle in the vegetable crisper. I hold my breath as I drag it out, hold it as far from my body as possible, dump it in the sink, then leave it to soak in cleaning liquid and water.

I clutch the broom and flee to the bedroom for some different air. It's empty but for dust balls and a couple of wire hangers on the closet floor. I pick up the hangers and sweep the dust into the hall. I return with the cleanser and water-filled pail, dip in a rag and wash down the walls where dry snot clings at bed height.

Then I tackle the bathroom, starting with the scum-layered tub. The toilet bowl is plugged with paper, tampons and shit. I won't reach into that, even with a rubber-gloved hand — I close the lid and leave it.

By the time I finish my first suite, Steve has finished three and he reminds me that we only have to do enough. I don't bother to tell him about the toilet. I lower my standards as I continue holding my breath through the next four apartments. Dried vomit. Rotten meat. Used condoms. Dead cockroaches left behind by the exterminators. The morning blurs.

The squatters on the second floor invite us for a cheese sandwich lunch and show off their cat who loves to chase tinfoil balls. They tell stories of last night's party in Steve's suite, stories that remind me of the ones, now faded in my memory, that I'd heard, maybe told, on Monday mornings in junior or senior high. I smile and nod my head pondering how their lives have turned out so differently than mine.

A few days later I meet up with Steve to collect my money, and as he counts out the twenties he tells me he'll be leaving the next day. Sometimes, when I sit sipping tea, I think of him running from the law — or other people who are much more sinister.

Pull Together

7 years old

My sisters and I have trouble sleeping on the nights we hear loud parties in full swing at the sand cliffs north of our house, but it's not the shouting or laughter or music that keeps us awake. On these summer nights, we wait for morning with almost the same sense of anticipation that we feel on Christmas Eve.

We eat our breakfast as fast as Mom will allow, no time for talk, then run out the door to search the yard for the red wagon, usually hiding somewhere behind the house or along the edge of the yard. Then we're off down the sandy path through the bush that leads to the cliffs. There is one big makeshift fire pit, surrounded by stones and logs, at the top of the cliff. We scan the trampled grass surrounding the still smouldering fire pit, on the lookout for the stubby brown beer bottles or soft drink bottles that we can exchange for cash.

We discover bottles in the pit, in the nearby woods, and at the cliff's edge, and load them onto the wagon until it can safely take no more. Then we take turns dragging and pushing as its wheels sink through the pine needles into the loose sand underneath. Clinking-bottle music rises up, competing with the wind and birds and cheering us on our journey home.

When we reach the house we box the beer bottles and beg Dad to take them in for us. We leave the soft drink bottles in the wagon for the trip to the store where we'll exchange them for penny candies or ice cream.

Twelve years later, my sisters and I are attending university in Winnipeg, living on student loans, bursaries and low paying jobs, sharing rent on a big old house across the back lane from a hotel bar. Most weekends we hold parties, inviting students who still live at home and who've nowhere else to hang out. The day after each party we cash in the beer bottles across the lane, buy a case for the next party, and save the rest of the money for what Mom taught us are the staples — groceries that are cheap, will last, and are filling: flour for baking powder biscuits, rice, macaroni, and potatoes.

Looking Down

"Look, look!" says Greta, her Dutch-accented voice loud and cracking. She's a refugee from an earlier generation of war. "She put the clean laundry on that dirty step."

Lena peers through the grime on her window. "And that's not the way to peg it either."

I pick another order from the stack, drop it on the paper-covered table under the window. I run my pen down the list: gowns, colour, size, stoles, caps, tassels. At the table next to me Greta also fills orders and further along Lena does the same. Shoulders hunched, heads bobbing, our hands repeat a task that will continue long after I leave this monotony.

I count and double check the ticked boxes, before I stop for a moment to glance out the window. It faces onto the back-lane of a residential area, home to many recent immigrants and refugees, that surrounds this old four-storey warehouse not far from downtown.

Three storeys below, I can see the woman standing on her back step. At her feet is a pile of wet laundry for hanging. She steps out from the shade, reaches for the clothesline. Then she turns, looks up and smiles. I smile too, not sure that she even sees me behind the sun's reflection. Her head is wrapped with a patterned scarf that I imagine was once stuffed in a battered suitcase. God knows what she's seen along the way.

There's no air conditioning. The drooping tail of clear plastic that I pull down to envelop the last maroon gown hanging on the hook clings to my bare legs, and I am a victim of static and sweat.

It's sad that a person's method for hanging laundry can be used by some people as the measure of that person. But I reason that I must work with these women, and I'll likely never meet the woman out the window. So I say nothing as I scoop a bunch of encased gowns from the rack and lie them flat on the table. Over and over I run my hand along the plastic, squeezing out the last bit of air, until I judge them smothered flat enough to fold and tape, ready for boxing.

No Time For Play

6 years old

I watch my oldest sister slog her way out to the frozen lake. The path that she's trampled into the snow with her daily trips is narrow, and she holds her arms out on either side to keep from falling over. She looks like a picture of the Lady Justice that I saw on a book cover, but instead of a scale and a sword she's carrying a pail for water and an axe. The axe is for knocking away the ice that freezes over the water hole every night.

This year, Mom and Dad have jobs on the east side of Lake Winnipeg, across the water and further north from where we usually live, so we're staying in a trailer. There's no electricity or running water, there's not even a well. It takes a while to adjust to oil lamps instead of light bulbs and to get used to hauling water from the lake. Mom saw a horse pooping in the lake so she makes sure to boil the water to kill germs before we're allowed to drink it. It always seems we run out of cold germ-free water right when I get thirsty. It takes forever for a new boiled batch to cool down.

Today my oldest sister's excited when she brings back the water. "Come here," she shouts, while she walks slowly to keep from spilling water on her leg. She's careful when she sets the pail down at the bottom of the trailer steps. "You gotta see this." She points into the pail.

I've been playing tag with some of my grade two classmates.

It's a cold day and my chapped lips are sort of stuck together. Some of the skin tears when I open my mouth to shout across the yard and it stings. "Okay, I'm coming." While I'm running I lick my lips even though Mom's told me it only makes the chapping worse — I can taste blood. But when I reach my sister and look down into the pail all thoughts of that are gone.

Something is moving in the water, gleaming silver in the sunshine reflecting on the inside of the tin pail. The fish is small and it looks like one of those sardines Mom likes to eat with raw onion a couple times a year. But this fish is alive. "What if he jumps out? What'll we do?" Before my oldest sister speaks the door swings open and Mom is on the top step. "Look Mom, she caught a little fish in the water pail! Can we keep him? He's so little, maybe —"

"No, you can't keep him. He has to grow up in the lake so you'll have to take him back. Hurry, I need the water for making supper."

I follow my big sister along the icy path and we don't talk. When we reach the water hole she gently tips the pail. Half the water is gone from it before the fish swirls down into the clear blue water under the ice.

Glass Bricks

They can be used for walls or windows, blocking sound and air, admitting only shadow light. They're strong, but they can be broken. I'm working demolition at an old warehouse that's being turned into a piano store, and I've never heard of glass bricks until my boss asks me to chisel them loose, breaking as few as possible, then hump them outside and up a long flight of stairs, four bricks at a time.

My arms and hands are numbed by the vibrations of hammer on chisel as I chip away at the cement that has held the glass bricks in place for years. I ride my bicycle across the city each day to work, so my leg muscles are already aching before I climb the scaffolding to loosen the bricks, climb down to stack them by the door, then run them up the stairs. And it's hot, so hot and humid, this summer. Back and forth, up and down I go, all damn day.

Late in the afternoon, when I round the corner one more time, carrying a box of bricks, I see a jogger on the sidewalk, his muscles running like rope up the length of his damp calves and thighs. The sweat on my forehead has turned the cement dust into mud and with my hands full I'm unable to wipe it away from my eyes.

Fuck you, I think, but I don't say it. You want to stay in shape? Why don't you carry some of these glass bricks up this flight of stairs? I'm sinking now, reaching my breaking point, almost stuck in the grey mud and he's just a guy running by.

Cleaning Always Seems to Be Involved

13 years old

Mom's cleaning schedule has nothing to do with necessity. I'm a teenager, and there is no satisfaction in sweeping a bare kitchen floor while the dust pan yawns in its corner. In wiping underneath lamps that when lifted leave no impression. In vacuuming a carpet with nothing caught in its pile. In a mop as clean when you finish as when you started. But it is not my satisfaction that matters.

Cleaning Music

The warehouse demolition and piano store renovation that I worked on all summer is almost complete, and the bosses, a married couple, lay off the guy who was hired two weeks before me. The husband tells me he was originally skeptical about a girl's ability to do such a physical job, but his wife convinced him — and she was right. In the fall, when I head back to university, they offer me a part-time job.

Once a week, I catch the bus in front of the university, make the long trip down Portage Ave. I vacuum, mop, and dust both the upright pianos and the baby grands.

I'm not a musician, polishing dull notes until they shine, or a dancer sweeping the room on tiptoe. But when there are no customers, and the bosses aren't around, I run my fingers over the keys and play Chopsticks, the only tune I've ever learned, notes dropping along with the dust.

Consider the Practical

7 years old

The water rises and flooding starts near our permanent home while we are temporarily living on the other side of Lake Winnipeg. When we return to our house we see that the lake is eating sand from the bottom of the cliffs along the shore. Trees sink and fall until their heads dip into the water and their roots are exposed along the beach. This action reveals fine grey clay that has been hidden underneath the sand.

One morning, I wander the beach, digging between the roots, packing the clay into a plastic pail. I carry the clay home to shape into pots and dishes on the front step. I fetch a basin of water from the pump and set it beside the clay I've collected. I dip and wet my hands so they can slip and slide to smooth the first blob into a dish. The dish seems to be missing something until I press my pointer finger to indent the rim, the same way our cousin's wife presses down on her cigarette to knock its ash into the teacup saucer Mom always places on the table when she visits. I have enough clay to fashion two more ashtrays before leaving all three to dry in the sun.

That night, I stand in the yard with my two older sisters, watching smoke try to erase the shower of ash and embers decorating the orange sky above the bush between our house and the burning house next door. By the time the volunteer firefighters arrive, the house is engulfed, and all they can do is water down the surrounding trees. When the fire is out, and the danger of it spreading to our house is gone, Mom sends us to bed. On my way up the front steps I see that one of the three ashtrays has cracked.

At dawn, my sisters and I rush through the trees to see what's left. My great aunt's cottage still stands, but all that remains of her son's log house is a fireplace, a chimney and the stone foundation running along the edge of its basement.

Back at home, I place my handmade ashtrays on the window ledge while I pour water over the step to wash away the extra clay. I discard the broken one in the grass along the edge of the garden. I overhear adults guessing at the cause of the fire. I think about cigarettes smoldering in tea saucers, maybe accidentally rolling to the floor. I put one ashtray in the drawer in Mom's dresser where I keep my art work and other treasures. I push the other one into the pocket of my shorts to keep safe. In the afternoon, I slip back down the path to the ashy remains of our cousin's house, and set the ashtray into a hollow in the foundation near what was once the entrance.

The following spring, my cousin and his family are living in another town. My great aunt plants seeds in the smoky basement shell of their house across the yard from her cottage. Vines climb up to carpet the blackened brick and stone. A mix of flowers fills the spaces between charred beams and stone and it becomes the secret garden I read about in a book borrowed from the shelves in her cottage.

I often sneak there to wander between cosmos and lilies. On hot dry days I worry about fires — a shiver of hairs crawling up my neck like an army of wood ticks — fires so easily started by wayward cigarettes. But I relax when I pass the indented ashtray, still safely perched in its hollow.

Contours

I think of the people who first generated all those lines on contour maps. Cartographers holding compasses out in front of their chests, pencils tucked between their fingers, leather satchels that trail bits of paper dangling from their shoulders. They hang off rock faces or spiral around mountains from foot to peak. They trek prairies and marshes, a boot or a bit of sanity lost somewhere in the miles between changes of elevation. Then they go home and hunch over desks — eyes squinted, brows furrowed, neck muscles taut — drawing lines and connecting numbers. Organized. Detailed.

While I work on my thesis, a demographic, socio-economic comparison, the university hires me as a geography lab assistant helping first-year students learn to read maps. I guide their fingers along the undulating webs that cross the unfolded pages. I explain the unruly circles and lines that run closer and closer together until they become tiny dots, mimicking rugged mountain tops. I show them how to trace V's, stacked like plastic cups lying sideways on kitchen shelves, pointing out rivers that long ago cut and snaked through shallow valleys. We smooth the paper where lines avoid one another, spreading like the prairie grass. Learning how to teach by teaching.

It's Not Always Easy to Rein It In

12 years old

No fence surrounds Mom's vegetable garden, yet nothing but her daughters dares stray beyond its edges. Dig. Plant. Thin. Weed. Hoe. Corn stands straight, tall, and evenly spaced. We slump over our dusty bare feet arguing with Mom about our need for free time: why do we always have to be working? Rows of pea vines lie in managed waves, but our uncombed hair tangles and frizzes. Potato plants give up treasures in one or two digs. Our secrets aren't so easily discovered. Ask. Pout. Demand. Threaten. Yell.

Inside the house, the harvest is malleable and easily controlled, unlike her daughters. Clean. Peel. Boil. Can. Freeze. Tomatoes nose up but can't break through glass sealer walls. We open bedroom windows and escape, along with smoky air. Beans don't challenge their fitted plastics bags, but our bodies spill out of halter tops and cutoffs. Carrots are sequestered in closed corner bins. Our words and actions aren't so easily constrained. Question. Argue. Push. Experiment. Rebel.

She taught us to read, supplying books, pencils, and pens. She prized our growing minds and good report cards. But a workforce exposed to words, opinions, thoughts, and ideas is not so easy to restrain.

Caught In A Cloud

Cumulus clouds have flat bottoms that sit at a height where water vapour condenses and the air becomes soupy. As the air warms up, they grow upward. The tops of these clouds can be rounded and cute like cotton candy or climb up and up until they turn into thunderclouds.

Lightning has just struck a flagpole when they call for me to board the float plane heading to a remote weather station in northern Saskatchewan. The pilot shouts over the din, says he'll try, but we might have to unload the soft drinks if the weight proves too much for takeoff. I'm trained to read the weather, then send that information to Winnipeg, but no one taught me how to die in a plane crash.

Vertical winds build within a thundercloud as cold air drops from the top and warm air rises from below. Water droplets are swept up and down inside the cloud, sometimes freezing in the top, then dropping to be coated by another layer of water, swept up again and frozen again, and so on. They can grow in size this way: quarters, golf balls, baseballs, until they weigh too much for the updraft and they fall as hail.

The boss at the weather station is not a happy man, lining up papers and pencils just so, like the always flat bottoms of cumulus clouds. On fair weather days, readings only need checking once per hour, leaving time for the bored devil on my left shoulder to out-manoeuvre the more mature angel on my right. I change the toilet paper roll from under to over, curious to see whether he'll put them all back on his next shift.

There are stories written about hang-gliders, para-gliders and parachutists, caught in a cloud-suck, swept up and down within clouds, bodies coated in ice.

At the end of the summer, on the flight out, I conjure a woman, perhaps me, in a cloud. Once the wind can no longer support her weight she's spit out and falls to the ground like hail. Maybe a man will find her and store her in his freezer until the camera crews arrive. Then he can appear on the news, standing beside his unusually large hail ball holding a metre stick for scale.

Patience Rewarded

5 years old

On Sunday mornings, our family sometimes visits my grandparents, Dad's parents, at their house. My grandmother, who we always call Lala, is usually in bed when we arrive, though not sleeping. One of these times I ask Mom why and, with a little sniff, she says my Lala wants to rest on Sundays.

Lala sits up in bed against two pillows, wearing a colourful dressing gown. She reminds me of a queen granting an audience to her subjects and I'm a little in awe of her. I stand still alongside my sisters because, though it's hard for me, over time I have learned that patience will be rewarded. If we behave Lala will soon point up at the shelf beside the door and ask my oldest sister to take down the painted tin box. "Open it up and get a candy for yourself and one for each of your sisters."

Opening the Car Door

While completing my Bachelor of Education degree, I get a summer job at a day camp working with groups of children who have been diagnosed with Attention Deficit Hyperactivity Disorder. We are based in a downtown community centre, but the children come from all over the city, so the Department of Education provides us with two cars in which we collect the children each day. Our job is to help the children learn to socialize with each other while doing arts and craft activities and swimming at the community centre pool. We also help them to learn appropriate behaviour in other public settings like movie theatres, museums, and swimming pools. The snacks we provide are healthy: we don't allow anything with sugar, chocolate, or additives.

We pick up the children, drive to the day's activities, and take them home in pairs because someone must be available to put out the fires while the other drives. There's always lots of noise in the cars, at our day camp, and at the buildings we visit: kids yelling at one another or at us, some crying, some repetitive banging, basically semi-controlled chaos. Sometimes, when I'm managing a child who is out of control on the street or at a museum, I catch people rolling their eyes or shaking their heads. I assume they think I'm the parent — a bad parent to have raised such an unruly child.

Carla jumps on my lap when we pick her up one morning and, while I turn my head for secret breaths of clean air, asks me why the other kids won't play with her. And I, having drawn the short straw at the camp staff meeting, have to make home contact to share our concerns about dried urine on clothing. The following morning, she opens the car door and tells me she washed her clothes all by herself late last night. I smell lemon dishwashing detergent and feel the dampness when she snuggles too close.

There is a story for every child, each one so fragile in their own way. In the morning, when I open the car door to let a child in, I don't know what I'm getting.

Rodger disappears one afternoon, returns spinning like the cartoon Tasmanian Devil, and admits he's eaten three chocolate-covered donuts at the day camp next door where there's no ADHD sugar-chocolate-additive ban. We're driving down the middle lane of Pembina Highway and he decides it's a good time to dive at the door and escape the car. I manage to pluck up a bit of his t-shirt and hang on.

Each time the car door opens I must hang on to my patience, but I learn a bit more.

Pushing Through

12 years old

I'm lounging on my bed reading *Jane Eyre,* and I hear Mom say, "The grass needs cutting." Somehow cutting the grass has become my job. Of course, I'm at the point in the book where the fire has just started. "I'll do it in a minute."

"Now!"

"Ahhh, Mom, I'm at a good part."

"Now!"

"Shit." I think I whisper it.

"I heard that, get out there."

I stomp my way to the side of the house where the rusty push lawnmower leans against the wall beside the recently-maimed gas lawnmower. No one would call the grass in our rural yard a lawn, though Mom has tried, pushing it and the gas lawnmower blades to their limits. It's just cut grass and weeds covering bumps and filling holes.

I pull the push mower to the sunny side of the yard, saving the shady area for when I need to cool off. Back and forth. Push. Push. Back and forth. I can see myself reflected in the picture window so it feels kind of surreal — an out-of-body experience. Back and forth. Push. Push. Back and forth.

The sun is close to the highest point in its arc through the sky. I'm sweating, my feet are stained green, and I still haven't reached the shade. Of course this spot I'm in is the most uneven section of ground. Back and forth. Push. Push. Back and forth. Stuck. Push. Push. Push. Stuck. Stuck. Stuck. I turn my head and watch my reflection pick up the push lawnmower. Then, like some sort of Olympic discus throwing champion, my reflection twirls and heaves it across the yard.

Mops, Envelopes, and Numbers

The summer after I graduate with a Bachelor of Education, I take a job with an organization that provides employment and training for young adults with mental health issues and intellectual disabilities. I spend part of each day demonstrating specific skills and the rest observing as the clients work on these skills.

The place has the cleanest washrooms in the city. The clients training as custodians shine mirrors, wash sinks, scrub toilets, and mop floors over and over. There is no dust on the office desks and carpets are pristine. Cleaning the same thing every day can be dull, but not as dull as watching people do it over and over.

Before the internet, businesses do a lot of bulk mailings. Stuffing photocopied sheets into envelopes is time consuming — not a cost-effective task for better-paid employees who are needed for more complicated things. I run my finger over a damp sponge, grab a page, fold it once, fold a second time, then slip it into an envelope while trying to avoid paper cuts. It's only a bit more exciting than watching people lined up along a table doing the same thing over and over.

In the small cafeteria upstairs we don hairnets and, after demonstrating the skills, I watch people wash dishes, hand out food, punch numbers into the cash register, and count coins for change. I watch this over and over and over.

Part 4

Using Every Work Skill You've Ever Learned

Teaching Junior High (1987 - 1994)

1

The girl slumps on the hallway floor in a practiced indifference near the classroom. Her eyes brighten when she sees me — holding a key aiming for the only door that matters right now. She must read me fast because the bell will soon ring.

Her eyes beam out a shifting ticker tape of thoughts. Is this a substitute who will follow the teacher's instructions — make us work? Or one who will sit at the desk hiding behind a newspaper while students text, gossip and apply makeup?

She stands — sees no newspaper. I push open the door and move to let her in. "Not my class, just waiting to say hi to a friend," she says — already marching her books and binder toward her locker.

2

Everything about Raymond is soft and pale, though I'm not certain this holds true for his memories. At first I can't understand why he mouths insults, just loud enough to be heard, at classmates much bigger than himself. And then a tough guy has him on the ground, kicking him in the head and in his soft stomach. I send the educational assistant for help, push in between them, take a few blows. Raymond lies there, bruises forming around the smile that now brightens his face.

3

I started smoking when was eleven. For my first ten years teaching, going for a smoke as the bells permit is practically my only break. There are still smoking sections in the staff rooms of the junior and senior high schools when I start teaching, but five years in, smoking is banned in public buildings and I'm forced to smoke outside until I quit another five years after that.

So, for these ten years, I smoke at home while I get ready for work. Then I smoke in my car all the way to school, storing up the nicotine in my body while preparing my smoke-free classroom for the day.

Right before the warning bell rings in the morning, I run to the staff room, or outside, for a cigarette with colleagues. We won't get another chance until the morning break, if we're lucky and no students need our help, or possibly until lunch. While I'm busy all morning with students my thoughts of cigarettes don't last long, but they're there.

When lunch bell rings, if no students need my help, I rush

to the staff room to eat lunch. If I don't have lunch duty or a meeting or work that needs immediate attention, I relax and have a couple of smokes with the other smokers, and a few non-smokers who like the boisterous smoking section atmosphere, before the afternoon warning bell sounds and it's time again for classes. But if I do have lunch duty or a meeting or work to do, I quickly smoke one cigarette and rush off hoping it'll be enough to get me through the afternoon.

When the 3:30 bell rings and most students have cleared out, except those needing assistance or those who would rather not return to unhappy homes, I run for a cigarette. I return to chat with lonely students or help them with school work or do some marking or facilitate a yearbook meeting or coach a team practice or a game or attend a staff meeting or meet with a parent. Then I smoke all the way home.

In the evening, on weekdays, I do marking, plan lessons or read teacher resource books, usually until midnight. I smoke like a fiend throughout. I take Friday nights and Saturdays off, but almost always do school work on Sundays.

Smoking, I tell myself, helps me relax when I'm feeling doubt and struggling with imposter syndrome, a constant for the first ten years of my teaching career. Without smoking, I tell myself, I couldn't possibly deal with the many layers of people in the education system. Large groups of teenagers. Parents. Other teachers. School and School Board administration. Provincial governments. And those members of the general public who, having once attended school, feel themselves to be experts with a strong need to share their strongly-worded opinions. So, for the first ten years, I smoke until the bell rings.

4

Mr. Mister is smiling today, a rare thing, as he enters the staff room, wanting to tell his story. He just gave his students a test. At the end of the class a girl handed hers in, most questions left blank, a frown on her face. *Mr. Mister, that test wasn't fair. It was too tough. I bet most of us failed it. Do you think we all have IQs of 100, or something?*

5

No matter how much you try you just cannot love everyone. You can hardly tolerate some of them. Jon comes to school every day, always late. He likes an entrance. Door crashing open, knob dinting the already dinted wall. *Well I'm here, I'm here.* Words sharp and burrowing.

On this day, Carl has come to school too, a rare occurrence. He must have something to sell. *Shut the fuck up.* But Jon keeps talking. Before I can cross the room the one-way punches are landing. I tug on Carl's shirt, trying to move him away, but it only rips. I plead for the two largest boys, sitting and smiling at the back of the room, to help me. They stand. Slowly. Move forward. Wait a beat. Then pull Carl from Jon.

6

September: Marvin's in Grade 7 and he refuses to write, won't even print something word for word from the overhead projector. *Just tell me a story out loud. Don't worry about writing it down.* He twists his stringy hair and shares an action movie plot. "This one cop is mad 'cause his wife was killed in a car accident so him and his cop partner are always fighting. They go to try and save this girl but her house explodes and stuff. Then a helicopter comes and kills a girl and there's a drive-by."

October: *Let's make a list of words you like. I'll print them, then you can copy them into your notebook.* He hikes up his pants that hang down, crotch at his knees. "Car. Crash. Fire. Gun." He tells me a joke about a gun and I laugh even though I don't get it.

January: Y*ou tell me some sentences and I'll write them on the paper.* "He has big muscles and a machine gun. He shoots at the car speeding at him. The car rolls over in the ditch." He copies them into his notebook.

March: *I'll help you write a story.* He tells me he's going to write a story by himself. No bugging his neighbour. No sighs. No trips to the washroom. He works for twenty minutes, then he calls me over. "The man his big and ugly and he punch the lady and the good man com and saf her The End." *Wow, this is great. I love it!* Marvin grins, picks up his pencil and waves me away.

I slip into the hall. I see a teacher walking toward me. I run to her. S*even months! Seven months! He wrote a story by himself for the first time today. It took seven months to get him to this point. It's about a man who saved a lady from the man who punched her.*

She smiles. *That's nice.* She teaches Grade 12 up on the third floor, where kids like him aren't likely to make it.

I sneak back and watch him through the doorway.

7

Allan catches my eye to let me know I haven't been giving him enough attention. He never talks to me, but likes me to talk to him. He's aged out of the special class for kids who have trouble coping in a regular classroom. So they've integrated him back into one — mine — and there's no educational assistant attached.

Right now, he's holding a chair over his head.

They chose this class. A mix of thirty-two students: a number of English as a Second Language kids, the brightest Grade 7 student in the school, another guy who regularly breaks out singing "Mickey Mouse!" when he forgets his medication, some kids who can barely read or write, a few students with behavioural issues, and a bunch of average students. And now him.

He's quiet, unlike the guy he has randomly chosen as his target today, but I can tell what he's saying. *I'm gonna bring this chair down on this guy's fucking head. I can't stop myself, but you can stop me.*

I cross the room, weaving around tables and desks.

8

Phone numbers are seven digits long because it's more difficult for the human brain to remember combinations of more than seven digits. The same applies when we're reading. If we read out loud or trace a finger under the words as we read, after seven words we must move on in order to process seven new words, often forgetting the previous seven. This makes it more difficult to comprehend what we read out loud.

But the brain is an amazing thing. If we read for the ideas, not worrying so much about the individual words, especially the small ones (the, and, with, as) we can get up to seven ideas, before we have to clear our minds, and we will remember more information.

I have just finished reading an article about this when a mother phones me, worried about her twelve-year-old daughter Nan's weak reading skills. Every night she has Nan read out loud. Although she reads very well, she can't answer questions about what she's read.

I explain the theory in the article and ask Nan's mother if she's willing to try letting her daughter read silently to herself.

A month later she contacts me again to tell me that Nan's comprehension has greatly improved.

9

Fight! There's a fight in the hall. I'm working at my desk because I have a preparation period right now. *Annie's nose is bleeding!* Annie is a new girl whose looks have attracted a little too much of the boys' attention. *A girl punched her.* There are other girls who want the attention of those boys instead. *You gotta come out here quick!*

I reach the door in seconds. Annie rushes into the room, blood dripping between the fingers she's holding over her nose. I send a student to get the nearest teacher with first-aid training. I grab paper towels from the side table and hold them over Annie's nose. Blood mixed with tears is soaking the front of her white T-shirt and the floor is getting slippery.

The other teacher swoops in and takes Annie to the office. A vice-principal, shouting for the students to clear the hallway, passes the door with the culprit in tow. It's all over in three minutes.

I wipe the blood off the floor in the classroom and the hallway, then wet a fresh bunch of paper towels in the washroom nearby and wipe the floor again. I tie the garbage bag closed and return to the washroom to soap and wash my hands.

Twenty minutes later, I open a drawer and spot the envelope with a few pairs of latex gloves and a brief memo explaining how, in the era of AIDS, we must safely deal with injuries involving blood. No tips, though, on the timing and inconvenience of the actual accidents.

A Year Off to Write (1994 - 1995)

1

Saturday at the Group Home

I'll sleep over at the group home every Saturday night until I find a better part-time job to supplement my income while I take a year off from teaching. The supervisor and I sit at a table and shuffle through the pages of a binder — reminders and anecdotes penned by the previous shift-worker, and blank pages left for me to fill.

We creak up the scuffed wood stairs to the third floor of this weary old house. There's a small room between two bedrooms — a closet really — with a locked desk. It holds the medications dispensed each evening and morning as well as a ledger to sign after the empty packets are discarded. The supervisor introduces me to the clients before she leaves.

Every shift, I show Lee magazines, suggest card games, talk about animals, trees, snowmen, anything to distract him. The distraction never lasts longer than ten minutes. He tells me his story over and over, always it's the girl from school, years ago. Lee is short and has bowed legs under his faded jeans. His combover can't hide the greasy shine of his scalp, the shine that spills down to his wrinkle-bumped face. Though his face has aged, his mind and the girl in it remain the same, stalled in classroom halls. Long blonde hair and a smile that I imagine was kind one even when faced with his bow-legged appearance. The word *unrequited* comes to my mind as he heads to the bathroom where he jerks off at least once each shift.

Harold is often standing in the foyer when I arrive, rocking, mumbling. He likes to drink tea and sometimes if I ask, he'll brew a pot and pour me a cup, the teapot dwarfed in his substantial hand. He's broad shouldered and tall — seems even taller because his brush cut, which is somehow always at the growing-out stage, almost sweeps the ceiling. We never have actual conversations because I'm the only one who speaks. Sometimes just mentioning tea sets off something in his mind, triggers a sequence of head banging, and all I can do is hold a pillow between his head and the wall.

Burt stays in his room, watching movies on his own television. He only comes out for meals which he douses with catsup until someone takes the bottle away. He eats candy, chips, chocolate bars and popcorn supplied by his parents during their brief weekday visits. His feet curl up in his shoes so he always limps, hands awkwardly scooping at the air to propel him forward. The one time I'm able to convince him to come outside for a walk he laughs at the snowflakes as they land on the sidewalk.

Shawna smiles when I dispense her birth control pill every Saturday morning. As she holds out her hand she babbles stories about a boyfriend I never meet, and giggles when I give her a bus ticket. Everything about her bounces — curly brown hair, plump tummy, light footsteps — when she heads off to spend the day, and usually the night, at this boyfriend's house. Often she comes home on Sunday mornings flush with money she can't explain.

2
Explaining Gatsby

Theme: Dissatisfaction. She is Mother, not Mom, never Mommy (*A+ A+ A A+ A+ A+ A+*). The missing +, like a space left in a row of teeth, sets hers on edge.

Theme: Class and Society. She did not send her son to Canada not to succeed, not to get into Canada's best medical school (*A+ A+ A+ A+ A+ A+ A+*). The only option is summer school and I'm hired to make sure he improves, fills in that blank space between A's.

Theme: Education. She arrives to stay for weeks, spends much of her time in the kitchen, grinding carrots and ginger into large glasses of juice for me, glasses replenished just when I am about to call it an evening (*A+ A+ A+ A+ A+ A+ A+*).

Themes: Lies and Deceit, Wealth. We study *The Great Gatsby*, page by page. His mother does not speak English, so he tells me his troubles between chapters and she does not know that she is paying for his therapy as well as buying (*A+ A+ A+ A+ A+ A+ A+*).

Themes: Love, Lies & Deceit. He meets a girl and he brings her up into the apartment one day when his mother is on a sudden trip back overseas to deal with a wayward daughter. He is in love, but he breaks up with her before his mother returns, so he can focus on his studies (*A+ A+ A+ A+ A+ A+ A+*).

Themes: Isolation, Religion. He is lonely, only allowed out for school or to attend services at the Mother-approved church. He asks me to the apartment almost every night, for company (not just *A+ A+ A+ A+ A+ A+ A+*) until I tell him I have a social life and can't work weekends.

Theme: Class and Society. He is broken-hearted, having trouble concentrating on his studies. He explains it is not that his mother is worried a girlfriend will distract (from *A+ A+ A+ A+ A+ A+ A+*). It's that though the girl is from their country, her father could never afford to play golf at the right country club.

Themes: Compassion and Forgiveness. His wayward sister arrives from overseas, an extended break from school. She sits on the couch, eyelids swollen from crying, until her brother finally gets his (*A+ A+ A+ A+ A+ A+ A+*) and into McGill. Her happy mother, before leaving to find an apartment in Montreal, hands her a ticket home.

Teaching Senior High (1995 – 2012)

1

This student is broad and tall and angry, must look down to look me in the eye. He's yelling, "Fuck you, bitch!" I have been working on myself: *I can't change you, but I can change how I react to you.* I tell him I'm sorry he's so upset, ask him to go into the hall, take some time and then we'll talk. Bewildered, he waits.

2

After months together, most students in this special class designed to help students who find it difficult to work in larger groups have settled down. But on this spring day, Trevor is causing trouble. He pokes a girl's back and when she turns he burps in her face. He peels an orange and throws bits at students across the room, who throw them back. He hums the Hockey Night in Canada theme over and over. Students plead with him, and then yell at him, to shut up.

I take a deep breath, then spot the lilacs out the window. "You know what, I'd love to have the scent of those lilacs in here. Students begin waving their hands. Trevor, why don't you go out there and get me some?"

He jumps from his seat and is gone before anyone can

complain about special treatment. I stay near the window. He soon appears out in the yard, turns, looks up at me and points to a nearby lilac bush. I shake my head at him, point to the furthest end of the yard. Behind me, everyone exhales.

3

When judges sentence young offenders to attend school in lieu of time in a detention centre, schools become jails.

As the bell rings for class change and students rush out and in, I can smell something burning. Before I can make my way out into the hall a student runs in holding the side of her head. "Someone came up behind me with a lighter. I didn't see who, but someone must have seen. There were people all around."

He waits in the hall, leaning against a locker, a small green disposable lighter in his hand. "It wasn't me. You can take me to the principal. I don't care."

He doesn't argue when I ask him to hand over the lighter. The other students move away as we walk to the office. They keep their eyes down. "I didn't do nothing. You can ask anyone if they saw."

4

A back lane shortcut — a jagged opening in the wire fence, a path across the football field, up cement steps and through the school's back door.

She sits at the back of the classroom and smiles to please foster parents and all the teachers. She does her best, but she's unable to control her impulses or understand consequences.

Every day she forgets — has to start over again — her fragile memory still floating like she once did in alcohol-tinged amniotic fluid.

In the winter she wears a new parka as white as the dirty-white snow. At first, one morning, the late stragglers crossing the field don't see her curled up on the frozen ground. She's passed out, smelling of beer. She might've frozen to death if these students had taken a different route. Consent or no consent, now inside her own drunk belly a new child floats.

5

Why does Manitoba have Louis Riel Day? Why was he hanged if he was a hero?

The senior high history curriculum involves teaching themes that involve critical thinking and discussion. But how do you start a discussion if kids have no background in these topics? You listen to their questions.

Why are some people mad about immigrants? When did we start having immigrants? What's the difference between an immigrant and a refugee? Is it fair for refugees to get in faster than immigrants?

What's a residential school? But we all have to go to school, don't we, so what's the problem? Why didn't they just not send the kids?

In that Great Depression, why didn't the government just print more money?

How come there isn't the same number of women in the government as men?

I back up and back up and back up until I get them to a familiar point and we take it from there. Try to move forward.

6

"It's not fair," says Jordan. He's complaining that he was fired from his part-time job at a major hardware store. This is not the first time I've heard these complaints. The student might change, but the stories are often similar.

"Why?" I ask.

"No reason. I missed a day. That boss's a jerk."

"They shouldn't fire you for missing a day. Did you call in? Did you miss any other days?

"Well... I guess I missed a few more days."

"Are you ever late? I know you're often late for class."

"Okay, okay... I guess I was late lots, but I can't help it that the bus always comes late!"

"What should you do if you find that the bus you take is always late?"

"Yeah yeah, take an earlier bus. But then I'm there, like, twenty minutes early."

And so the discussion goes.

Potential employers often say that young people are lacking basic work skills and educators are trying to respond. Like each teacher in our school, I lead an advisor group of students for whom I monitor attendance, keep in contact with parents, hand out and discuss report cards, assist with future course selection, and teach the skills needed for the school to work transition: resumes, job interviews, methods to access information, worker's rights, and — most importantly—basic work skills.

Mindy recently sneered at my suggestion that she look up a word in the dictionary, asking, "How can I look it up if I can't spell it?" Today, once the group has finished listing basic work skills, I ask everyone to now list skills they may already have learned — skills that can be transferred to the work world. "I don't have any work skills 'cause I never worked before," Mindy says.

"That's a good point, Mindy. Can you learn these kinds of skills anywhere else?"

A Note on Sources

The names of the people in these stories have been changed, with the exception of Barbara Stoppel ("Solo Night Shift"), and Tracey Walsh ("I Will Not Give Him A Name"), whose stories were reported by local newspapers and online media. Tracey Walsh insisted on having her name made public following the arrest of her rapist. Information about these women and their stories was found in Colleen Swifte's article, "Tracey Walsh fights the good fight..." Interlake Enterprise News, July 12, 2012.

"Teenager murdered, innocent man jailed: Excerpt from ex-Winnipeg detective's book." CBC News, August 9, 2017. https://www.cbc.ca/news/canada/manitoba/stoppel-excerpt-book-1.4239384

"Winnipeg woman to face rapist after parole hearing." CBC News, August 29, 2006. https://www.cbc.ca/news/canada/manitoba/winnipeg-woman-to-face-rapist-at-parole-hearing-1.592059

Acknowledgements

My appreciation to the publications in which versions of some pieces appeared: *Prairie Fire, Lemon Hound, Our Times,* and *Flash: The International Short-Short Story Magazine.*

I'm grateful to Ahniko, Conni, Heather, and Kelly, the current For Words writing group members, for unwavering support, humour and generosity, and the way you put up with my enthusiastic yapping. And thank you to the past members, as well.

Thanks to the poets and audience members of Speaking Crow, the long running open-mic poetry reading institution in Winnipeg. Many of the stories in this book started as poems that I shared on the first Tuesday of the month.

Thank you so much to At Bay Press. Matt Joudrey, publisher, for being kind and supportive. I will never forget the feeling of opening that acceptance email while riding a Winnipeg Transit bus. I looked around at the other passengers, buried in their phones at that moment, knowing none of them had better news than me. Rachel Burlock, editor, for being calm, sensitive, and insightful; Karen Clavelle, copy editor, for the attention to detail; Matthew Stevens and Matt Joudrey, for the great book design and layout.

Thanks to Kimmy Beach, who helped me shape the MS and decide it was prose. I really enjoyed our chats, too.

And finally, thank you to my friends and family who come to readings, read my writing, and listen to me when I'm happy or sad. Especially James, who gives me quiet and steady support. And June, who always — always — has my back.